UNITED STATES
OF AMERICA

TIGER BOOKS INTERNATIONAL

Text
Patrizia Raffin

Translation
Richard Reville

Graphic design
Patrizia Balocco

Contents

2-3 One of the most spectacular spots in Utah, which in terms of natural wonders is second to no other state in the U.S.A., is Bryce Canyon, a huge abyss which opens up on a fir-covered plateau at an altitude of 8,200 feet.

4-5 The New York skyline stands out against the horizon. The panorama of United States metropolises is characterized by skyscrapers, which have become famous for their particular architectural forms.

6 A cowboy having a break at sunset beside a giant cactus is one of the most common images of the West: a man, his horse, and nature.

7 Like solitary, majestic giants, the high natural reliefs of Monument Valley loom over a desert rendered arid by the burning sun. The Navajo Indians, who once lived on this land, gave these imposing natural towers strange names which were sometimes infantile and rather irreverent.

8-9 The Preservation Hall Jazz Band is one of the symbols of New Orleans' musical tradition.

10-11 San Francisco at night is lavish with lights and promises thousands of after-midnight entertainment opportunities, as one might expect from such a lively city which is so symbolic of a certain part of the west coast and so free from social prejudice.

12-13 Daytona Beach, in Florida, is 24 statute miles long and is frequented by young people who arrive in unusual vehicles. The sandy base is so compact that cars and motorcycles can be parked almost down to the water line.

14-15 Oak Alley is the most famous plantation in Louisiana. Built in 1750 by a family of French origin, it is approached along a splendid drive lined by centuries-old oak trees whose trunk circumference is, in some cases, equal to 33 feet.

This edition published in 1993 by TIGER BOOKS INTERNATIONAL PLC , 26a York Street Twickenham TW1 3LJ, England.

First published by Edizioni White Star
Title of the original edition:
America, il Paese del grande sogno.
© World copyright 1992 by Edizioni White Star.
Via Candido Sassone 22/24, 13100 Vercelli, Italy.

ISBN 1-85501-299-5

Printed in Singapore
Color separations by Magenta, Lit. Con., Singapore.

26 top *The night traffic on San Francisco's Golden Gate Bridge traces brilliant "cables" of light.*

26 bottom *The intersecting of many thoroughfares reminds one that it is impossible to live without a car in Los Angeles. Only with an automobile can one cover the enormous distances which separate the different parts of this megalopolis.*

27 top *Lombard Street, in San Francisco, forms ten hairpin curves which are edged by flower beds full of hydrangeas.*

27 bottom *Speed limits on American roads are rather low, and the maximum limit is 55 mph. This picture shows the highway which goes to Atlanta.*

28-29 *A seaplane cuts through the waves in Miami, Florida.*

30-31 *In spite of the recent competition from Atlantic City, Las Vegas remains the world's most popular gambling spot.*

paradoxically, America relates and expresses itself also in the adult amusement park of Las Vegas, along the mile-long street known as "the Strip," the most brightly illuminated street in the world, whose dazzling multi-colored signs can be seen at distances of up to 60 miles. The origin of Las Vegas' wealth is the result of a Nevada state law which, beginning in the 1930s, enabled couples to obtain a divorce within a few weeks and made it equally easy to speed up the procedures for getting married. Thanks to these facilitations, an army of people wanting a divorce flew into Las Vegas, which prepared itself to welcome them with thousands of slot machines, innumerable blackjack tables and, in short, all the instruments which permitted the wait for the divorce to be passed pleasurably. Since then, the capital of entertainment has added other strings to its bow, diversifying the offers provided by its excellent restaurants, casinos and hotels which host world famous stars. The tourist can choose between the Bacchanal Room, which reproduces a Roman villa from the times of Augustus, in Caesar's Palace Hotel, the Gigi Cafe in the MGM Hotel, which simulates the interiors of the costume film "Marie Antoinetta," or even the Carson City Restaurant in the Circus Hotel, where the diners sit around an arena in which trapeze artists, clowns, and acrobats perform. The majority of money changes hands around traditional tables of dice, blackjack or roulette or is played in slot machines, video poker machines, and video formula one races as well as competitions against robots which have been electronically programmed to make things challenging. Gambling, which is favored psychologically by the absence of clocks and windows so as not to give the players any rest, remains the real protagonist and brings to the city and to Nevada more than two billion dollars a year. The fact that Las Vegas is preparing to become an important convention center in the 1990s is the result of that typical American business sense, but, for most people, it remains the city of gambling and intends to remain so for a long time to come.

Death Valley is about 130 miles from Las Vegas, on the borders of Nevada and California. In its Dantesque landscape, the presence of man is merely an accessory. Here, nature is the protagonist, not only because of the unusual beauty of the landscape, which includes the gold and purple of the Golden Canyon, the ochre of Mustard Canyon, the red, green, and brown of the Black Mountains and the multi-colored pebbles of the Mosaic Canyon, but above all because of the solemn and almost lunar atmosphere which the natural elements created about three million years ago, between the end of the Pliocene period and the beginning of the Quaternary era. Here, erosion by atmospheric agents and huge volcanic eruptions have created an infinite series of reliefs. Some of these are rocky and jagged like Artist's

Palette while others are more rounded like the dunes which color the horizon with yellow, orange, mother of pearl, and ochre. There are darker brushstrokes where the plants with very deep roots form flashes of color in an arid universe which still palpitates, lives, and forcefully imposes its beauty. Death Valley extends over an area of almost 7,000 square miles in the Mojave Desert. The Indians originally called it Tomesha (Land of Fire) and it was given its current name after the tragic event which happened to a group of gold diggers who succumbed to the infernal heat of the desert on their way to California in 1849. Yet, despite its funereal name, the hidden charm of this valley are to be found on starry nights when the heat lets up and the valley's numerous inhabitants come into the open; among these are goat antelope and wild mules which are the descendants of those famous convoys of 20 mules which brought sodium borate out of the valley at the time of the pioneers. There are also many species of birds including geese, heron, and ducks which visit the small marshes to be found in this vast territory. Human presence in the happy desert, as it has been defined, is very low and there are only 200 residents, the majority of whom are employed in the national park or in one of the two hotels in the region. Human intervention has been limited by the "impossible" climate, with summer temperatures of more than 50° C, but perhaps an intelligent limit has been placed on the use of the territory, and, with due respect to the natural treasures, country roads and structures have been built only where necessary.

America has always felt that its greatest richness was its territory, protagonist of so many western films, that land where palefaced horsemen hid themselves behind the pinnacles of Monument Valley, or rode on mules from one side of the Grand Canyon to the other, traveled up and down the wide prairies of the West, and hunted for bounty to the southwest in the Sonora Desert. Therefore, the United States began to preserve its natural resources from the more evil inhabitants when the concept of ecology had not yet been formulated. Indeed, in 1872, Yellowstone Park became the first national park in the country's history. A park with 200 geysers and 3,000 hot springs, waterfalls, and streams, terraces of travertine stone, swamps and stalactites, thousands of animals including bison, deer, elk, marmots, eagles, and falcons, on display against a backdrop of extremely varied natural beauty almost as if Yellowstone were trying to offer in its 9,000 square miles a sample of all natural marvels. Every year the park is visited by millions of people, and the risk of commercialization is thus very high, but for the moment the characteristics of Yellowstone have been maintained by the people who work in this sector.

Another precaution, albeit a little late, forbids the

collecting of fossils in the Petrified Forest Park, in Arizona. This area of 143,000 sqaure miles contains the largest collection of petrified wood in the world, and here the only color which does not appear is green. The desert landscape may seem inhospitable, consisting as it does of dead trees which have been turned into stone, but it has its own particular beauty and especially in the giant logs the magnificent colors highlight the incredible process of petrification, which began 70 million years ago and which caused the trunks to color themselves as splinters of onyx, agate, and jasper. Once again, it is Arizona which contains perhaps the most famous national park in the U.S.A., the Grand Canyon National Park. Of the 19 canyons which follow the course of the Colorado river from its source in the Rocky Mountains to its mouth in the Gulf of California, these 1,930 square miles contain the most spectacular geological structures, whose projection and shape are due to the erosion of the sedimentary strata which the river created five or six million years ago. The dominant colors are, as one might imagine, ochre and sienna, and the shapes bear witness to the forces of nature which modeled them in a few moments of unheard-of thrusting or by means of a slow progression which has lasted millions of years. Everything speaks of the greatness of nature, and those who do not like technical calculations and scientific explanations can place their trust in the almost mystic emotion which the sight of the Grand Canyon provokes, especially those who observe it from above, from an airplane or a helicopter.

On the border between Arizona and Utah we find that which cannot exactly be defined as an American park, but which quite rightly claims the title of an Indian Park – Monument Valley. In fact, it rises at the heart of the Navajo reserve, and it is the Indians who offer their services as guides for trips into this valley which contains the splendid formations of red sandstone, the peaks of which are more than 984 feet high and which suddenly rise up from the surrounding flat desert and have formed the background to so many Western films. These natural "towers" are equal in form to the buildings of Manhattan, and probably the two opposing images equally attract the interest of the tourist or of those who like to travel at home in the mind and create their own America.

On the other hand, America is in equal measure the frenzied world which throngs in the densely populated quarters of such metropolises as Chicago, Los Angeles, and New York, and that large, spacious country which has space to sell to those who want to travel across it and experience it. The United States is such a composite and complex reality that it would be impossible to try to classify it into well defined categories. There is a working America consisting of world-famous factories

which boast highly advanced production systems, and there is a poor America which lives in squalid ghettos thanks to the handouts of the welfare system or at the mercy of exploiters in the slums. There is the America of West Point with its cadets in their white uniforms and the country of the huge peace marches; there is the America of television "serials" and more conventional "soap operas" and the America which listens to itself in the poetry readings of avant-garde artists. There is the America which lives with the break-up of the family and the America which is attempting to regain higher values through the proliferation of numerous religious sects; the robust and slightly coarse America of the rodeo and other great sporting occasions and the America which burns up its young generations. The United States is a cross-section of varied humanity of opposing mentalities which overlap in a contradictory fashion. America is everything and the opposite of everything, and if we were to play the game of free association starting with the words "United States of America," it would be very difficult to bet on how many would say "Manhattan" and how many would say "Grand Canyon."

A Country Without Frontiers

"America is also and above all open space. Large, boundless, wild stretches portray the innermost sense of the country—the Grand Canyon, a chisel of rocky sculptures of breathtaking beauty, and the Rocky Mountains, with their legends of trappers, bears, Indians. And on another lyrical side is Hawaii: a most varied nature, with the palms of Oahu, the beaches and lagoons of Waikiki, the luxuriant vegetation of Maui, the volcanoes, and the warning wrecks of armed ships in the deadly waterways of Pearl Harbor. Forests are to be found throughout the country, as well as plenty of wild beaches with flying birds and sprinklings of foam. Coral reefs run along the islands. And unprofaned glaciers are common in Alaska, turned into the last frontier for oil, the American Siberia."

Guido Gerosa

In 1938 John Ford discovered the incomparable scenario of Monument Valley, and in 1939 this was the setting for his masterpiece *Stagecoach*. It was not only the great success obtained from both critics and public which caused Ford to come back here to film *Fort Apache* in 1948, *She Wore a Yellow Ribbon* in 1949, *The Searchers* in 1956, and *Cheyenne Autumn* in 1964. In his films, the landscape was the absolute co-star alongside the cavalry soldiers and the fleeing Cheyennes. The fact that Ford repeatedly chose Monument Valley is extremely significant and highlights the spectacularity of this natural scenario in which gigantic cathedrals of stone rise up loftily from the tormented ground.

32 top and 33 *The heights of Monument Valley have particular and rather surreal names which were given them by the ancestors of the 30,000 Navajo Indians who still live here and do not want to leave.*

32 bottom *Landscapes sculpted in the rocks cover large areas of the American West. Twisting gorges form the beds of thousand-year-old rivers and bear witness to the remote geological process which produced the wild beauty of the Grand Canyon.*

The Valley of Stone Cathedrals

Landscapes which are literally sculpted into the rock cover the wide spaces of the American West. Twisting gorges, crossed by millenarian rivers' flow, bear witness to the remote geological processes which created the wild beauty of the Grand Canyon. The spirit which animated its creation seems to have remained imprisoned in the monolithic blocks of Monument Valley. Indeed, the most beautiful songs of the Navajo culture speak of the origin of the universe and of that force consisting of rain, wind, and lightning which molded the rocks and desert.

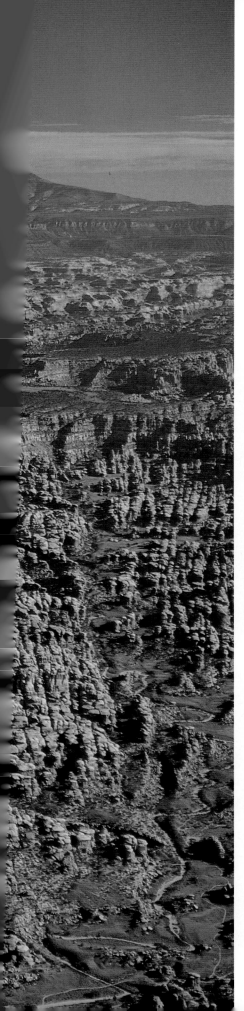

The Long Work of the Centuries

36-37 *Canyonlands National Park extends for more than 250,000 acres in the state of Utah.*

37 top *The San Juan River as it enters Gooseneck State Reserve in Utah.*

37 bottom *An aerial view of Lake Powell and the Glen Canyon National Recreation Area in Utah.*

38-39 *The Grand Canyon, which President Theodore Roosevelt defined as "that superb panorama which every American should see," was formed by the erosion carried out by the Colorado River over the course of 30 million years. In addition, the United States contains many other spectacular landscapes created by the tireless action of nature.*

The Everglades, an Endless River of Grass

The region of the Everglades extends over an area of 1,300 square miles characterized by grassy stretches, swamps, and a rather hostile nature. In 1947, a national park of 2,300 square miles created. This is constantly patrolled by a well-trained corps of rangers who guarantee protection to a number of animals, including the manatee and the heron, which seem to be threatened with extinction.

Alaska, the Kingdom of Perennial Glaciers

Alaska has been quite rightly defined as the land of records. It is dotted with three million lakes; its "skeleton" consists of tens of thousands of islands and at least 270 glaciers which were formed in ancient times. Its clear skies are crossed by 9,000 aircraft; Alaska has an airplane for every 50 inhabitants and a pilot for every 42. The distances here are enormous, and overland travel is very difficult, especially in the colder season. The territory of Alaska extends over an area of 595,000 square miles, which is twice the size of Texas and equal to a fifth of the entire United States. From 1799 to 1867, this immense land, with its wealth of natural resources, was under Russian dominion before being sold to the Americans for about $7.2 million. In the second

half of the last century, during the gold rush, Alaska was taken by storm by adventurers who dreamed of obtaining wealth quickly and easily. Among the pioneers, there was also a young writer destined for fame and glory – Jack London. In his stories he informed the world of the extraordinary uniqueness of these endless glaciers. Alaska is without doubt a strange country, dominated by enormous expanses of unpolluted tundra and taiga, in which caribou and wolves live in a self-regulating equilibrium which requires no human intervention. It was precisely for this reason that two million hectares were transformed into the Denali Nature Reserve, 248 statute miles south of the Arctic Circle, at the foot of the imposing mass of the 20141-feet-high Mt. McKinley.

Cities

"It is the fascination of the great American megalopolises which captures our imagination more than anything else. The influence of cinema and television have made Manhattan and Los Angeles seem more familiar to a young Italian than his home town. We can recognize the spire of the Chrysler skyscraper, or the house Frank Lloyd Wright built for Kaufmann, the Golden Gate and Brooklyn Bridges, and the Guggenheim Museum because they have been impressed on our mind's eye through the images of films, music and the photographs of *Life*."

Guido Gerosa

American cities, unlike European ones, are not linked to a well-defined and centuries-old history. However, their characters are nonetheless evident to the many ethnic groups who have had a part in their development, whether examined from the point of view of the very rich or the very poor.
Most of the cities pulsate with life, and echo to the sounds of the ever-present traffic, mingled with the voices of all the different peoples who have adopted the place as home.

64 top *The best view of the city of Seattle is to be had from the top of the rotating restaurant known as the Space Needle.*

64 bottom *The 4th of July celebrations in Philadelphia have a fundamental importance for every citizen. The celebrations are commensurate with the role this city played in the nation's history. In fact, the Declaration of Independence was signed at Philadelphia in 1776, and for a certain period, the city styled itself with the title of Capital.*

65 *The Empire State Building and the more recent World Trade Center, whose twin towers soar heavenward in the background, are among the best known symbols of New York.*

New York,
The Big Apple

"It's unique: its neuroses, its fever, its streets, which are dirty but luminous, smelly but perfumed, elegant but tumble-down, are the marvels of the world."

Guido Gerosa

84

Boston, The Cultured City

Boston has been called the most European city in the United States, and when one strolls along Arlington Street where the rich Bostonians built their beautiful mansions and majestic churches, one realizes what is meant by European atmosphere. Here, where the Boston of Henry James maintains its characteristics, there is no exhibitionism nor a false note to disturb the harmonious equilibrium of the city.

New Orleans, City of Joy

The city whose emblem contains an old-fashioned grand piano clearly demonstrates its great love for music. However, this banner also reveals something else about New Orleans. The piano recalls the resistance offered by this confederate city in 1863 against the northern forces under General Sherman. The artillery of the Washington regiment placed this musical instrument in the

center of the fray and, accompanied by its notes, sang old patriotic songs before and after the attacks. The urban layout and the architectural style of the buildings are evident signs of the French and Spanish domination which alternated until 1803, when Napoleon sold the city to the United States of America. The most famous and certainly the most fascinating zone of the city is the Vieux Carr, the French Quarter, on the right bank of the Mississippi, which saw the birth of jazz at the start of the 20th century.

Dallas, The Rich "Big D"

Perhaps it is Dallas which holds the record for stereotypes in the United States. The image which springs to mind is that of the super-rich Texan with a cowboy hat who manages his many petroleum companies from the top of a modern glass skyscraper and who travels by Cadillac to reach his ranch just outside the city. This is partly true, since statistically, Dallas has the greatest number of luxury automobiles in the Western world, and the standard of living is quite high when compared with other cities, which have terrible areas of misery. It should, however, be remembered that oil alone is not sufficient to guarantee wealth and that behind a splendid landscape there is a productive reality based on hard work.

Miami, Millions and Art Deco

The most heterogeneous society in the United States is to be found in Miami. In particular, Cubans and Mexicans form a high percentage of the population, and it has indeed been estimated that half of the entire population speaks Spanish. Geographically, the city is divided by Biscayne Bay into two zones connected by the numerous highways and bridges which cross this stretch of internal sea.

From above, the surface of the water seems to be dotted with artificial islands on which there are luxury villas with private jetties and berths. Along with Miami Beach, Miami benefits from the wealth brought in by the tourist industry which has developed here thanks to the tropical climate and the luxuriant vegetation. Over the years, the city has created infrastructures which have no equal elsewhere in the world, with more than 500 hotels, 400 motels, and more than 4,000 restaurants. Many of these complexes were built by rich Cubans who fled their homeland between 1959 and 1960 with the fall of the Batista regime. In Little Havana, they have partially recreated the charming atmosphere of their country, developing one of the most picturesque corners of the city, pleasantly in contrast with the bright lights and modern architecture of the luxury hotels.

Honolulu, Paradise Regained

On the beaches of Waikiki, when King Kamehameha I conquered the territory of Oahu in 1795, the vegetation extended down to the shoreline, and in the surrounding area there were many fields interspersed with inhospitable swamps. Now, years later, the panorama has radically changed, and this beach has become one of the most representative symbols of international tourism.

Some 120,000 people live in an area of no more than 1.1 square miles, in which there are about 450 restaurants and 1,000 shops. The mythical Eden which nestled at the foot of Diamond Head, the extinct volcano which has become the symbol of Hawaii, has been transformed into a modern, rich, and cosmopolitan tourist paradise in which ancient traditions and customs, modified to serve the imperative needs of market and economy, struggle to survive. An eight-lane highway connects the airport to the city, and it is constantly full of traffic. At Honolulu, everything is geared to promoting the tourist industry, which is without a doubt the most important economic activity on the island and the principal source of employment for its inhabitants.

A Style of Life

"Every city and town in America is a world. The people in the United States have a multi-faceted dimension. A boundless planet and a human constellation without end which has undergone a ceaseless process of transformation in the last twenty years and is a source of joy to sociologists, observers of customs, narrators, and film directors.

Raymond Cartier has written that there are fifty Americas, one for every State of the Union. And it's true. The people are like chameleons. At every hour of the day they change skin and color and show themselves in different styles and fashions."

Guido Gerosa

It is not possible to give a single definition to the American style and way of life. One can speak generically of a style of life without presuming to include all aspects of the same. The United States contains an infinite variety of ethnic groups, each characterized by different histories, sentiments, and temperaments. The one thing they all have in common is a deep love for that country which unites and represents them.

96-97 One of the images which most often springs to mind when speaking of the United States and its people is that of the cowboy: those skilful herdsmen who live in direct contact with nature, far from the compromises and the intrigues of business and the chaotic traffic of the large cities.

98-99 There are many different competitions in a rodeo, and they are all spectacular. The cowboys skilfully ride bareback or tame wild horses in a short time. They also wrestle with steers and compete in capturing calves using a lasso.

Lazy like a summer in Los Angeles but frenzied like Wall Street, America offers both of its faces to those who wish to get to know it. The fable of Uncle Scrooge McDuck, who created his fortune starting off with a nickel, has been surpassed today. There remains the capitalistic taste for accumulating and increasing economic well-being and the force of a professionalism reached by dint of hard work.

104-105 *Wall Street is America's economic temple. It is here that the fortunes of the country are created and consolidated, and it is here that the strings of the world are pulled.*

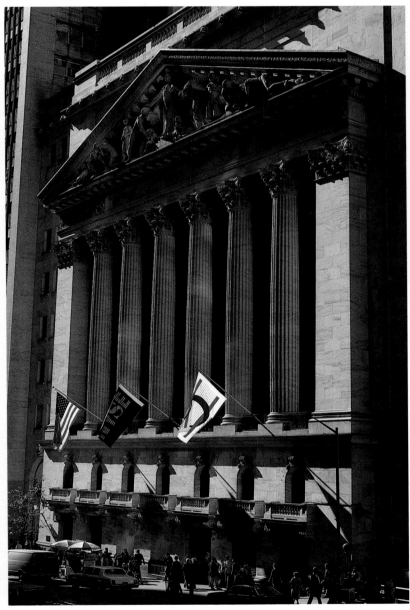

A Nation for Sport

Sport is the principal source of amusement, hobby, and pleasure relaxation in the United States. Millions of fans watch and practice a wide range of sports with great passion. Many of them also play, at an amateur level, those same sports which they admire in the large stadiums.

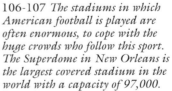

106-107 *The stadiums in which American football is played are often enormous, to cope with the huge crowds who follow this sport. The Superdome in New Orleans is the largest covered stadium in the world with a capacity of 97,000.*

107 left *American football players take to the field wearing light suits of "armor" which are necessary because of the violence of the game.*

107 right *Basketball also has many fans, not only because of the overpowering superiority of American teams in international competitions, but also because children play it in schools from a very early age.*

108-109 *Baseball is the quintessential American sport. Its origin dates back to the initiative of Alexander Cartwright in the last century, but the definitive rules were not laid down until 1859. The picture shows the Los Angeles stadium, in which the Dodgers have excited millions of spectators with their exploits.*

109 top *The oldest hippodrome in the U.S.A., the Saratoga Race Track, has become part of the myth of American society in the same way as Wimbledon is a legend for the United Kingdom. During the racing season, this small city comes to life and becomes the place where the exponents of high society must be seen.*

109 bottom *Golf is a very popular sport in America, and there are many excellent courses with a very high technical level.*

109

110 Sailing is the most practised sports in coastal regions. In this picture a sailboat approaches the Golden Gate Bridge at San Francisco.

110-111 In the United States all sports are loved and followed in a more or less intense manner, and occasions for creating and watching spectacles are always welcome. This photograph shows a large gathering of hot-air balloonists in Albuquerque, New Mexico.

The Art of Living

To say that entertainment was born in the United States is certainly excessive, but to claim that the Americans know how to enjoy themselves more than any other people is certainly not an exaggeration. The wide open spaces and the extraordinary natural beauty represent a remarkable starting point, but this would all be worth nothing without the spirit, enthusiasm, and organizational ability of which the inhabitants of the United States constantly give proof. A family holiday in a camper, the magic of Disneyland, an improvised show at Ghirardelli Square in San Francisco, or an important date in Hollywood, everything, really everything in America is a unique occasion not to be missed and to be lived to the fullest.

112 *An American family enjoys the sunset on a splendid beach in Florida.*

113 *The camper is the vehicle which is most commonly used to take the family on holiday, and perhaps, as in this case, to search for the most charming corners of Florida.*

114-115 *Daytona Beach, Florida is thronged with people year round because of the mildness of the climate.*

Palm Beach owes its birth and development to Henry Flagler, a rich railroad magnate and business partner of the Rockefeller family, who realized the potential of this area as a residential center in 1893 and convinced some of the best known families in the country to move to the south. Within a short time Palm Beach became the preferred residence for members of the high society, and it then developed inexorably. Today North Avenue, with its refined boutiques offering the most exclusive creations of international designers, is considered the most opulent street in the eastern United States.

118-119 *If Palm Beach offers a pleasant climate and crystalline water for a serene old age, the natural calm of Georgia proposes a valid alternative for those who wish to enjoy moments of authentic tranquility.*

A human jukebox along the streets of San Francisco, a tightrope walker who performs at sunset on the pier at Key West, and students playing music in the main square at Berkley University are all different aspects of a unique way of living and searching for spectacle in daily life. In the United States every spot, square, or crossroad is the ideal place for putting oneself on show, certain that one will manage to attract an attentive and well-disposed audience. America is really the world of spectacle, but at the base of this singular characteristic there is a deep respect for the individual and of his right to express himself even in non-conventional ways, as long as it is not offensive to the dignity of others.

122-123 *Disneyland is in Anaheim, California, 27 miles from Los Angeles on the west coast, and Disneyworld is in Orlando, Florida on the other coast of the United States. Disneyland was created by Walter Elias Disney in 1955, responding to the secret expectations of millions of children and adults. Disneyworld was its continuation 15 years later, enriched quite rightly with a better and more modern concept of an amusement park.*

124-125 *Despite the fact that the epoch in which Hollywood was famous all over the world has long gone, every tourist who visits Los Angeles tries to visit the sidewalk on which the stars have left their handprints and buys a ticket for Mann's Chinese Theater. Here one can relive the atmosphere of the great cinemas of the 1940s, which, with their bas-reliefs, stuccoes, and brocade stage curtains, were temples for the magical rites of showing films that provided the dreamstuff for entire generations.*

The Pioneers of Space

There are three space centers in the United States. The least known is in Alabama, and the more famous ones are the Lyndon B. Johnson Center at Houston, Texas, and the John F. Kennedy Center in Florida, formerly known as Cape Canaveral. Splendid American organization has made it possible for all those curious about space travel to visit the launching pads in all three centers. It is also possible to see perfect reproductions of the Apollo lunar modules as well as to try out mission simulations such as those in which the astronauts train for future missions. This work of promoting space activity has the aim of making the entire nation share in the great progress and the conquests which have been made in this sector, which presents itself as a new frontier, a challenge to the innate pioneering spirit of the Americans.

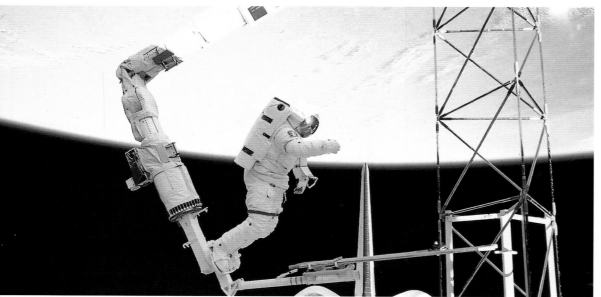

126 top left *Sophisticated instruments are capable of controlling, from earth, the missions in space.*

126 top right *The shuttle taking off from the launching pad is a spectacle of true technological power.*

126 bottom *Vaguely disturbing technological advances are at the base of progress and space conquest.*

127 *The lunar adventure is now history in the United States. Aeronautical engineering has enabled the achievement of goals which until a few years ago seemed inconceivable.*

128 *American flags outside a bar in Key West, Florida.*

Photo credits:

Marcello Bertinetti/Archivio White Star:
Pages 8-21; 22 bottom; 24-29; 40-49; 55 bottom; 56-61; 62 top left and center; 63; 71 top; 72 left; 72 bottom right; 74-77; 78 top left, bottom left, top right; 79; 82-83; 84 top; 85 bottom; 86-87; 90-93; 100; 102-103; 105 right; 106; 107 left; 108-111; 113-115; 116 bottom center; 117; 119-121; 122 top; 123-125; 128.

Angela White Bertinetti/Archivio White Star:
Pages 62 bottom; 78 bottom left; 112; 116 top; 118.

Peter Adams/Stock Photos/ACE:
Pages 80-81.

Apa Photo Agency:
Pages 23; 32 top; 66.

Armstrong/Zefa:
Page 6.

Dallas & John Eaton/Apa Photo Agency:
Cover; pages 1; 54; 55 top; 64 top; 67-70; 72 top right; 84-85 center; 98-99; 105 left.

Ben Dregon/Animals Animals/Overseas:
Page 96.

J. Dressel/Zefa:
Page 32 bottom.

Robert Knight/Apa Photo Agency:
Pages 30-31; 53.

Dennis Lane/Apa Photo Agency:
Page 101 top.

Ben Nakayama/Apa Photo Agency:
Pages 126-127.

A. Nate/Overseas:
Page 107 right.

Stan Osolinski/Overseas:
Page 55 center left; 55 right.

David Ryan/Apa Photo Agency:
Pages 50-51; 78 top; 94 right.

Blair Seitz/Apa Photo Agency:
Page 64 bottom.

R. Gomez/Zefa:
Page 97.

R. Strange/Apa Photo Agency:
Page 94 left.

Adina Tony/Apa Photo Agency:
Pages 22 top; 34; 35 top; 52; 111.

Adina Tony/Overseas:
Pages 88-89.

John Warden/Overseas:
Page 101 bottom.

Perry Alan Werner/Apa Photo Agency:
Pages 73; 104.